Rails Ac
Rannc

CORROUR
SUMMIT

1350ft (411m)

ABOVE SEA LEVEL

ISBN 978 0905 489 92 6
Published by Famedram Publishers Limited, PO Box 3, Ellon, AB41 9EA
© Copyright 2013 Famedram Publishers Limited www.northernbooks.co.uk
Strictly no reproduction in whole or part without written permission
All colour photographs © Famedram; b&w, courtesy Scottish Records.
Print: Imprint Digital

Overleaf: Into the hills on the climb to Tyndrum

Rails Across Rannoch

Highlights of the rail route from Crianlarich to Fort William

Bill Williams

Northern Books
from Famedram

Belt and braces – a steam excursion arrives at a sunny Crianlarich, with Class 37 diesel backup in close attendance. Just visible behind 61994, the famous Crianlarich tearoom, still offering the traveller a warm welcome.

The old and the new at Crianlarich. The Great Marquess on steam excursion duty (above) and, right, a service Sprinter bound for Glasgow.

Fort William's aluminium smelter provides welcome freight traffic on the line

A long line of Rio Tinto Alcan wagons hauled by a Class 66 diesel at Crianlarich

The Great Marquess sets off tender first to Oban on a rescue mission for a stranded steam excursion.

Crossing the Fillan, with storm clouds gathering over Ben More

On its way to Fort William, to begin the summer's Jacobite run to Mallaig and back, 62005 passes Inverhaggernie crossing just north of Crianlarich. The Fillan viaduct can just be seen in the distance.

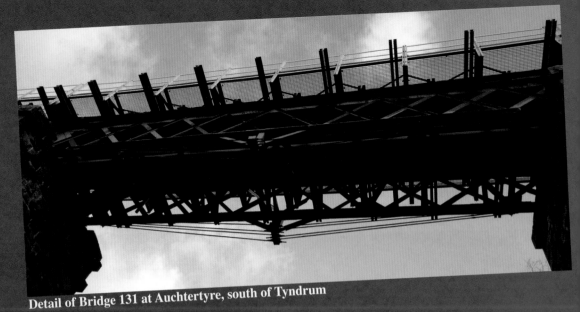
Detail of Bridge 131 at Auchtertyre, south of Tyndrum

As soon as it got into mountainous territory, the West Highland line provided challenges a'plenty to its builders.

Though none of them might seem particularly mighty, even the most modest rivers could call for some pretty daunting bridging.

Unlike the later Mallaig line where concrete was the favoured (and at the time revolutionary) medium, on the West Highland steel was chosen, supported on soaring, elegant stone piers.

At Auchtertyre, Bridge 131 carries the line effortlessly across the river far below as it climbs towards the gold rush village of Tyndrum.

Massive stone piers carry the line high above the river

A morning Sprinter train climbs into the hills en route for Tyndrum (next stop) and Fort William.

The Great Britain V luxury steam excursion train crosses Bridge 131, high above Auchtertyre, a popular provisioning stop for walkers on the West Highland Way, on its journey to Fort William and Mallaig.

Maybe not gold, but there was lead in them thar' hills – spoil from earlier mine workings in the hills above Tyndrum, visible from the train shortly after it leaves Upper Tyndrum travelling north.

The changing face of a Highland rail halt – Tyndrum Lower has graduated from the homely garden shed (above) to the weird variations on a bus shelter shown right and below.

The name may change, but the station stays the same. Tyndrum
Upper becomes Upper Tyndrum (to avoid confusion with Tyndrum
Lower) but it's still a long haul up the windy road from the village.

Ruined lineside cottage with Beinn Dorain (1076m/3503ft) catching the early morning sun as it overlooks the celebrated horseshoe bend at Auch.

After Bridge of Orchy the West Highland line starts the adventure proper of crossing the deserted waste of Rannoch Moor. Having kept fairly close company with the main road from Ardlui, the line climbs towards Rannoch in the heart of the moor, while the road goes almost due north to Kingshouse and Glencoe.

For miles on end there is no road access anywhere near the line and there are precious few tracks even. Hence the need for dual purpose road/rail vehicles like the one above for the maintenance crews who are often based here.

Bridge of Orchy lies bang on the route of the popular West Highland Way. Indeed the official route uses the concrete underpass which also provides access to the island platform of the station

Bridge of Orchy is one of the best maintained of the Swiss chalet style stations on the line. The station was converted to a bunkhouse and for a short while this use also supported a restaurant

Now you see it, now you don't – Gorton's passing loop came and went (top picture) and came again (middle and bottom pictures). Some eight miles north of Bridge of Orchy, a small railway community once existed here, with a school in a converted carriage on the platform and, in the early days, some railway cottages nearby. It was never really a station – the mighty Breadalbane Estate did not welcome visitors – and today little evidence of any past activity at all remains.

All that remains of the old Gorton stopping place today. What is left of the old platform can just be made out between the two sheds.

Gorton marks the start of the Moor proper – a 400 square mile morass of peat bogs, stagnant pools, stunted bushes and heather. The great road maker Thomas Telford surveyed a route across it for a road – and then thought better of it.

Across the Moor few bridges of any size were needed. That crossing the River Gaur, shown looking north towards Rannoch (top) and south (above), was a rare exception. The real problem for the line's builders was finding a firm footing for the track. They solved this by piling a mass of brushwood into trenches, then in-filling with excavated rubble and ashes,

Apart from the ubiquitous scrub and heather and the odd plantation of conifers, there is precious little natural vegetation to be seen across the Moor until a (rare) settlement comes into sight. Rannoch station is surrounded by trees, as is the neighbouring hotel, the lonely Moor of Rannoch Hotel, seen above.

As inaccessible stations go, Rannoch is not quite in the premier league. It does have a public, tar road to it and is clearly marked on maps. But it is still quite a trek. Make your windy way off the A9 Perth-Inverness road to Kinloch Rannoch, stop for a breather there and then continue the 18 switchback single track miles to Rannoch station. Depending on a number of variables, you *might* be able to enjoy a well-deserved cuppa in the station tearoom, once voted one of the best in Brita

Local communities and businesses have been encouraged to take over redundant station builings on the West Highland and establish alternative uses. One enterprising manager of the t room saw the potential for the development of an interpretive centre for the line (and the Moor) the former waiting room and it's a job that has been well done. It's well worth taking in.

While we still have a functioning mail service covering *all* of rural Britain you can in theory also post a letter on the platform here... but remember, last (and first) post goes at 11am

Waiting room as interpretive centre. Illustrated panels on the wall tell the story of the line and the challenging country it passes through.

This way to the hills. The line climbs north out of Rannoch towards the highest point reached, at Corrour some eight miles farther on.

An eloquent tribute to a saviour of the line. A funding crisis for the West Highland was averted by the generosity of one director, James Renton, who came up with a vital injection of funds. This huge head at the north end of Rannoch station was carved by grateful workers.

A major challenge to the line's builders came just north of Rannoch station where the longest viaduct on the line – nine spans covering 684 feet – carries the line across some of the most difficult terrain. Deep excavations were called for before a sound footing could be found in the treacherous bog below.

After Rannoch the line climbs for the last stage of the journey across the Moor to the highest point on the line eight miles farther north at Corrour. Though the terrain is somewhat less treacherous, it can still be pretty bleak and inhospitable. No shelter of any sort is afforded across the barren landscape.

No sooner had the West Highland finally been completed than a new hazard emerged – the harsh Highland winter. As luck would have it the very first winter after the line opened was the harshest of the century. The line was blocked for days on end. The answer: snow fences – the remains evident above – and a snowshed, the only one on a British line.

Corrour at last! Not journey's end by any means, but the worst of the Moor conquered and some shelter and, possibly, welcome sustenance.

Not only Britain's remotest station, not served by any public road, but also the highest and surely the only one with its own wind generator?

A steam special, left, waits for a Glasgow bound Sprinter (top) to pass before beginning the descent to Loch Treigside – and Fort William.

Originally built as a private station, Corrour has latterly been known to boast both a restaurant and bed and board – and a sunny welcome, but best to check first.

Scene at the foot of Loch Treig during construction. Following damming of the loch in 1937 the line had to be diverted and raised some 10m.

Hard (and soft) hats of assorted hue for a boat party at work on the West Highland line

Pre-portakabin site accommodation on Loch Treigside – complete with full complement of staff

The Lochaber smelter hydro scheme in the 1930s called for damming and raising the level by some 10m of Loch Treig (left). This called for a 2km diversion and a new tunnel (top), only the second one on the line.

ridge inspection for the bridge over the River Spean, just up river from Spean Bridge village itself

More than a century later, the same bridge, holding up well, seen prior to a much needed paint job

PLEASE HAVE
ALL TICKETS
READY

Left, stylish enamel sign from earlier times, still very much in evidence at Spean Bridge long after all traces of British Railways (and any station staff) had gone.

Above: Spean Bridge's listed brick built signal box amid the carefully manicured topiary and, top, rare visit of a Class 37 diesel, making a welcome change from today's ubiquitous Sprinters.

Less than a dozen miles to go now from a sunny Spean Bridge to journey's end at Fort William.

Rainbow's end – rainbow over Fort William greets another steam special
after safely negotiating the challenge of the rails across Rannoch Moor.